Deutsch-Lotto

A Fun Way to Reinforce German Vocabulary

Colette Elliott and Michaela Greck-Ismair

Brilliant
PUBLICATIONS

We hope you and your pupils enjoy playing the lotto games in this book. Brilliant Publications publishes many other books for teaching modern foreign languages. To find out more details on any of the titles listed below, please log onto our website: www.brilliantpublications.co.uk.

100+ Fun Ideas for Practising Modern Foreign Languages in the Primary Classroom	978-1-903853-98-6
Das ist Deutsch	978-1-905780-15-0
Wir Spielen Zusammen	978-1-903853-97-9
German Pen Pals Made Easy	978-1-905780-43-3
German Festivals and Traditions	978-1-905780-52-5
¡Es Español!	978-1-903853-64-1
Juguemos Todos Juntos	978-1-903853-95-5
¡Vamos a Cantar!	978-1-905780-13-6
Spanish Pen Pals Made Easy	978-1-905780-42-3
Lotto en Español	978-1-905780-47-1
Spanish Festivals and Traditions	978-1-905780-53-2
Chantez Plus Fort!	978-1-903853-37-5
Hexagonie 1	978-1-905780-59-4
Hexagonie 2	978-1-905780-18-1
Jouons Tous Ensemble	978-1-903853-81-8
C'est Français!	978-1-903853-02-3
J'aime Chanter!	978-1-905780-11-2
J'aime Parler!	978-1-905780-12-9
French Pen Pals Made Easy	978-1-905780-10-5
French Festivals and Traditions	978-1-905780-44-0
Loto Français	978-1-905780-45-7
Giochiamo Tutti Insieme	978-1-903853-96-2
Lotto in Italiano	978-1-905780-48-8

Published by Brilliant Publications
Unit 10
Sparrow Hall Farm
Edlesborough
Dunstable
Bedfordshire
LU6 2ES, UK

Sales and stock enquiries:
Tel: 01202 712910
Fax: 0845 1309300
E-mail: brilliant@bebc.co.uk
Website: www.brilliantpublications.co.uk

General information enquiries:
Tel: 01525 222292

The name Brilliant Publications and the logo are registered trademarks.

Written by Colette Elliott and Michaela Greck-Ismair
Illustrated by Gaynor Berry
Front cover designed by Brilliant Publications

ISBN 978-1-905780-46-4

First printed and published in the UK in 2009

Contents

Introduction

The perennially popular game of lotto is an enjoyable and effective way to teach and/or reinforce vocabulary and language structures. It can be used as a teaching tool or as a fun follow-up activity after a lesson. It provides a stimulating and meaningful way to develop reading, listening and speaking skills.

The games in *Deutsch-Lotto* can be played in a variety of ways (see pages 5–7) and with very little preparation from you. There is no need to give the children counters or individual cards. Simply photocopy the boards, hand them out to your pupils together with some colouring pencils and, bingo, you can start playing!

Our unique call sheets provide the 'order of call' and enable you to follow the game closely and to select which team you want to win.

Lotto can be played in small groups, or with an entire class. There is no limit to the number of players and the games are suitable for ages four upwards.

There are seven topics in *Deutsch-Lotto*:
- Die Zahlen 1–12   Numbers 1–12
- Die Zahlen 1–60   Numbers 1–60
- Tiere   Animals
- Essen   Food
- Im Klassenzimmer   Classroom objects
- Kleidung   Clothes
- Weihnachten   Christmas

For each topic there are three versions of the boards, allowing maximum flexibility, particularly in mixed ability classes.

pictures only

words and pictures

words only

The ideas in this book are by no means exhaustive and, should you decide to cut the boards to make flashcards or playing cards, then the number of games is unlimited!

Have fun playing!

How to play

Getting started

For each topic, in each format, there are four different numbered boards, so you can play with four teams. Just photocopy the sheets, cut them in half, and hand out the boards to the children. For a class of 28 pupils, you only need to copy two pages seven times each.

It is a good idea to go through the vocabulary with the children before playing. The best way to do this is either to scan and place the four boards on the whiteboard, or enlarge the 12 pictures on the photocopier and use them as flashcards.

Make sure that the boards are evenly distributed throughout the class. After giving the boards out and before you start playing, ask for a show of hands to see how the teams are spread out in the classroom. The children like to see who is in their team and this increases the element of competition!

How to play

Each topic contains a call sheet, with the words numbered 1 to 12. The caller can start calling from any number. The white area in the table indicates who the winning board will be.

The children can play on their own or in pairs for moral support.

The winner is the first child to shout 'lotto' (hopefully the rest of that team will also shout 'lotto', but the real winner is the child who shouts out first). Get the winner to say all the words in German whilst you check on the list. This is a good reading/speaking exercise.

Once the first team has won, you can stop the game or carry on until everyone has shouted 'lotto' (you will know from the call sheet who the next winner will be).

You can play several games with the same boards by marking the boards in different ways:
◆ Colour the box outline (or only one side of the box if you want to make it last!)
◆ Colour the picture
◆ Colour the background
◆ Tick or cross the box, etc.

It is best to tell the children to shout 'lotto' as soon as the caller says the word, rather than wait until the colouring is done, to avoid any arguments.

Variations

Instead of evenly distributing the boards, you could make it a competition within the class: divide the class into four groups, give the same boards to each group, and see which group says 'lotto' first.

Children could play in groups of five. One child is the caller (give him/her a photocopy of the call list) and the others use four different boards. Only one winner this time!

The order of call is the same for all the topics, so you can play 'mix and match' games with different topics. If you decide to do so, make sure that the four different teams are evenly spread.

Different ways of playing/ideas

◆ Call the words from the call sheet in German. Start anywhere, but make a note of where you started either on a photocopy of the call sheet or on a separate sheet of paper. Alternatively, get a child to do the calling. Assist him/her with the more difficult words

◆ The children take it in turns to call out an item from their own board in German. When they call a word, they colour their own picture and everybody who has that picture says 'danke' and colours their picture. Then the child sitting next to the caller says the next word, etc. This is a very good reading exercise if the 'words only' boards are used. The teacher should make a note of which items have been called on the call sheet.

◆ Call the words in English, and the children have to find the German translation (this can only be played with the 'words only' boards).

◆ Show a picture without saying anything (using the 'words only' boards).

◆ Write a word on the board without saying anything (for 'pictures only' boards).

◆ Instead of using the call sheets, photocopy the boards and cut them up into cards, then pick the cards out of a hat. The pupils could take turns to pick a card and call out the word.

◆ Ask the children to colour the pictures before playing and then call the words with a colour, eg "Eine rote Katze". To keep the game from lasting too long, limit the children to the same two colours. (You can use the two columns on the call sheets to indicate the colour. For example, write B for "blau" at the top of the list of German words and R for "rot" at the top of the English word list.)

◆ Give a description of the word in German.

◆ For the number "lotto" boards, give sums for the children to work out.

◆ Spell the words.

◆ Give a rhyming word.

◆ Include the word in a sentence eg Bonbons; Bonbons, bitte; Ich möchte gerne Bonbons, bitte; Guten morgen, ich möchte gerne Bonbons, bitte.

◆. Make the game last the whole lesson. Give the boards at the beginning and call the words at intervals during the lesson, either on their own or in a sentence.

◆ Give everybody the same board. Each child has to preselect four items by circling or colouring them.

◆ Give the children the blank template board (pages 57) and get them to write/draw their own items/numbers from a list you have given on the board. This can be played with any topic/ structures/verbs/grammar.

◆ Make the children repeat the word several times whilst they are colouring.

◆ The children ask a question each time, eg:

✳	Was möchtest Du gerne?	What would you like?
✳	Wie viele? Welche Anzahl? Welche Anzahl hast Du?	How many? What number? What number do you have?
✳	Was ist das?	What is this?
✳	Was isst Du gerade?	What are you eating?
✳	Hast Du ein (Haus-) Tier?	Do you have an animal/pet?
✳	Was ziehst Du an?	What are you wearing?

◆ If you photocopy the boards double-sided, they will last even longer.

Die Zahlen 1–12

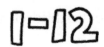

Team 1 to win	Start on 2 or 7
Team 2 to win	Start on 1, 3, 4 or 12
Team 3 to win	Start on 3, 5, 7, 10 or 11
Team 4 to win	Start on 5, 7, 8 or 9
All teams to win	Start on 6

These numbers refer to the numbers on the left and right of the grid below.

Tick the white boxes in the grid as you call out the words.

Order of call			Winning team												
			2	1	2&3	2	3&4	All	1,3,4	4	4	3	3	2	
1	fünf	five													1
2	neun	nine													2
3	elf	eleven													3
4	zwei	two													4
5	vier	four													5
6	zwölf	twelve													6
7	drei	three													7
8	eins	one													8
9	sechs	six													9
10	acht	eight													10
11	zehn	ten													11
12	sieben	seven													12
1	fünf	five													1
2	neun	nine													2
3	elf	eleven													3
4	zwei	two													4
5	vier	four													5
6	zwölf	twelve													6
7	drei	three													7
8	eins	one													8
9	sechs	six													9

Lotto! (Spielbrett 1)   Name: _____   1-12

2	8	9
3	1	4

Lotto! (Spielbrett 2)   Name: _____   1-12

1	5	6
4	12	2

Lotto! (Spielbrett 3)   Name: _____   1-12

7	5	10
11	3	4

Lotto! (Spielbrett 4)   Name: _____   1-12

11	4	6
7	8	9

Lotto! (Spielbrett 1)

Name: _____

1-12

2 zwei	**8** acht	**9** neun
3 drei	**1** eins	**4** vier

Lotto! (Spielbrett 2)

Name: _____

1-12

1 eins	**5** fünf	**6** sechs
4 vier	**12** zwölf	**2** zwei

Lotto! (Spielbrett 3)

Name: _____

7 sieben	**5** fünf	**10** zehn
11 elf	**3** drei	**4** vier

Deutsch-Lotto – Die Zahlen 1–12

Lotto! (Spielbrett 4)

Name: _____

1–12

11 elf	**4** vier	**6** sechs
7 sieben	**8** acht	**9** neun

Deutsch-Lotto – Die Zahlen 1–12

Lotto! (Spielbrett 1)

Name: _____

1-12

zwei	acht	neun
drei	eins	vier

Lotto! (Spielbrett 2)

Name: _____

1-12

eins	fünf	sechs
vier	zwölf	zwei

Lotto! (Spielbrett 3)

Name: _____

$1-12$

sieben	fünf	zehn
elf	drei	vier

Lotto! (Spielbrett 4)

Name: _____

$1-12$

elf	vier	sechs
sieben	acht	neun

Die Zahlen 1–60

Team 1 to win	Start on 2 or 7
Team 2 to win	Start on 1, 3, 4 or 12
Team 3 to win	Start on 3, 5, 7, 10 or 11
Team 4 to win	Start on 5, 7, 8 or 9
All teams to win	Start on 6

These numbers refer to the numbers on the left and right of the grid below.

Tick the white boxes in the grid as you call out the words.

						Winning team									
			2	1	2&3	2	3&4	All	1,3,4	4	4	3	3	2	
1	sechsundzwanzig	twenty-six													1
2	sieben	seven													2
3	sechzig	sixty													3
4	fünfunddreißig	thirty-five													4
5	achtundfünfzig	fifty-eight													5
6	einundvierzig	forty-one													6
7	fünfzehn	fifteen													7
8	fünfzig	fifty													8
9	zwölf	twelve													9
10	zweiundvierzig	forty-two													10
11	vierunddreißig	thirty-four													11
12	neunzehn	nineteen													12
1	sechsundzwanzig	twenty-six													1
2	sieben	seven													2
3	sechzig	sixty													3
4	fünfunddreißig	thirty-five													4
5	achtundfünfzig	fifty-eight													5
6	einundvierzig	forty-one													6
7	fünfzehn	fifteen													7
8	fünfzig	fifty													8
9	zwölf	twelve													9

Order of call

Lotto! (Spielbrett 1)   Name: _____   1-60

35	42	7
15	50	58

Lotto! (Spielbrett 2)   Name: _____   1-60

50	26	12
58	41	35

Lotto! (Spielbrett 3)　　Name: _____　　1-60

19	26	34
60	15	58

Lotto! (Spielbrett 4)　　Name: _____　　1-60

60	58	12
19	42	7

Lotto! (Spielbrett 1)   Name: _____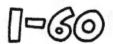

35 fünfunddreißig	42 zweiundvierzig	7 sieben
15 fünfzehn	50 fünfzig	58 achtundfünfzig

Lotto! (Spielbrett 2)   Name: _____   1-60

50 fünfzig	26 sechsundzwanzig	12 zwölf
58 achtundfünfzig	41 einundvierzig	35 fünfunddreißig

Lotto! (Spielbrett 3)

Name: _____

19	26	34
neuzehn	sechsundzwanzig	vierunddreißig
60	15	58
sechzig	fünfzehn	achtundfünfzig

Lotto! (Spielbrett 4)

Name: _____

60	58	12
sechzig	achtundfünfzig	zwölf
19	42	7
neunzehn	zweiundvierzig	sieben

fünfund-dreißig	zweiund-vierzig	sieben
fünfzehn	fünfzig	achtund-fünfzig

Deutsch-Lotto – Die Zahlen 1–60

Lotto! (Spielbrett 2)   Name: _____   1-60

fünfzig	sechsund-zwanzig	zwölf
achtund-fünfzig	einund-vierzig	fünfund-dreißig

Lotto! (Spielbrett 3)   Name: _____   1-60

neunzehn	sechsund- zwanzig	vierund- dreißig
sechzig	fünfzehn	achtund- fünfzig

Deutsch-Lotto – Die Zahlen 1–60

Lotto! (Spielbrett 4)   Name: _____   1-60

sechzig	achtund- fünfzig	zwölf
neunzehn	zweiund- vierzig	sieben

Tiere

Team 1 to win	Start on 2 or 7
Team 2 to win	Start on 1, 3, 4 or 12
Team 3 to win	Start on 3, 5, 7, 10 or 11
Team 4 to win	Start on 5, 7, 8 or 9
All teams to win	Start on 6

These numbers refer to the numbers on the left and right of the grid below.

Tick the white boxes in the grid as you call out the words.

				Winning team												
				2	1	2&3	2	3&4	All	1,3,4	4	4	3	3	2	
Order of call	1	ein Schwein	a pig													1
	2	eine Maus	a mouse													2
	3	ein Meerschwein-chen	a guinea pig													3
	4	eine Kuh	a cow													4
	5	ein Hamster	a hamster													5
	6	ein Pferd	a horse													6
	7	ein Kaninchen	a rabbit													7
	8	eine Katze	a cat													8
	9	ein Hund	a dog													9
	10	ein Goldfisch	a goldfish													10
	11	eine Ente	a duck													11
	12	eine Henne	a hen													12
	1	ein Schwein	a pig													1
	2	eine Maus	a mouse													2
	3	ein Meerschwein-chen	a guinea pig													3
	4	eine Kuh	a cow													4
	5	ein Hamster	a hamster													5
	6	ein Pferd	a horse													6
	7	ein Kaninchen	a rabbit													7
	8	eine Katze	a cat													8
	9	ein Hund	a dog													9

Lotto! (Spielbrett 1)

Name: _____

Deutsch-Lotto – Tiere

Lotto! (Spielbrett 2)

Name: _____

Deutsch-Lotto – Tiere

Lotto! (Spielbrett 3)   Name: _____

Lotto! (Spielbrett 4)   Name: _____

  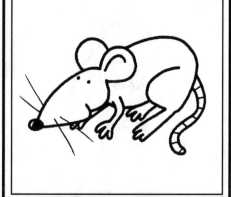

Lotto! (Spielbrett 1) Name: _____

 eine Kuh	 ein Goldfisch	 eine Maus
 ein Kaninchen	 eine Katze	 ein Hamster

Lotto! (Spielbrett 2) Name: _____

 eine Katze	 ein Schwein	 ein Hund
 ein Hamster	 ein Pferd	 eine Kuh

Lotto! (Spielbrett 3)   Name: _____

 **eine Henne**	 **ein Schwein**	 **eine Ente**
 **ein Meer-schweinchen**	 **ein Kaninchen**	 **ein Hamster**

Lotto! (Spielbrett 4)   Name: _____

 **ein Meer-schweinchen**	 **ein Hamster**	 **ein Hund**
 **eine Henne**	 **ein Goldfisch**	 **eine Maus**

Lotto! (Spielbrett 1)   Name: _____

eine Kuh	ein Goldfisch	eine Maus
ein Kaninchen	eine Katze	ein Hamster

Lotto! (Spielbrett 2)   Name: _____

eine Katze	ein Schwein	ein Hund
ein Hamster	ein Pferd	eine Kuh

Lotto! (Spielbrett 3)   Name: _____

eine Henne	ein Schwein	eine Ente
ein Meer-schweinchen	ein Kaninchen	ein Hamster

Lotto! (Spielbrett 4)   Name: _____

ein Meer-schweinchen	ein Hamster	ein Hund
eine Henne	ein Goldfisch	eine Maus

Essen

Team 1 to win	Start on 2 or 7
Team 2 to win	Start on 1, 3, 4 or 12
Team 3 to win	Start on 3, 5, 7, 10 or 11
Team 4 to win	Start on 5, 7, 8 or 9
All teams to win	Start on 6

These numbers refer to the numbers on the left and right of the grid below.

Tick the white boxes in the grid as you call out the words.

Order of call				Winning team												
				2	1	2&3	2	3&4	All	1,3,4	4	4	3	3	2	
1	ein Kuchen	a cake														1
2	ein Apfel	an apple														2
3	ein Eis	an ice-cream														3
4	(etwas) Käse	(some) cheese														4
5	ein Hähnchen	a chicken														5
6	eine Kartoffel	a potato														6
7	(etwas) Milch	(some) milk														7
8	(etwas) Schinken	(some) ham														8
9	ein Ei	an egg														9
10	Pommes Frites	chips														10
11	(etwas) Brot	(some) bread														11
12	Bonbons	sweets														12
1	ein Kuchen	a cake														1
2	ein Apfel	an apple														2
3	ein Eis	an ice-cream														3
4	(etwas) Käse	(some) cheese														4
5	ein Hähnchen	a chicken														5
6	eine Kartoffel	a potato														6
7	(etwas) Milch	(some) milk														7
8	(etwas) Schinken	(some) ham														8
9	ein Ei	an egg														9

Lotto! (Spielbrett 1)   Name: _____

 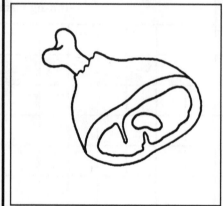 

Deutsch-Lotto – Essen

Lotto! (Spielbrett 2)   Name: _____

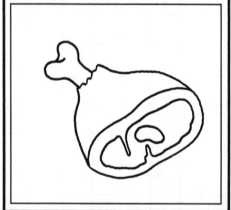  

Lotto! (Spielbrett 3)   Name: _____

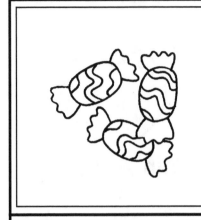  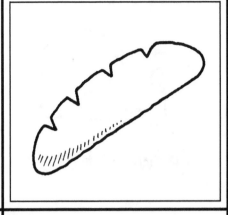

Lotto! (Spielbrett 4)   Name: _____

Lotto! (Spielbrett 1)

Name: _____

(etwas) Käse

Pommes Frites

ein Apfel

(etwas) Milch

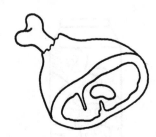
(etwas) Schinken

ein Hähnchen

Lotto! (Spielbrett 2)

Name: _____

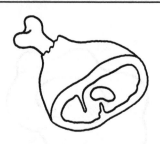
(etwas) Schinken

ein Kuchen

ein Ei

ein Hähnchen

eine Kartoffel

(etwas) Käse

Lotto! (Spielbrett 3)

Name: _____

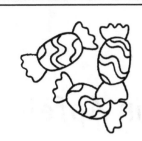		
Bonbons	ein Kuchen	(etwas) Brot

ein Eis	(etwas) Milch	ein Hähnchen

Lotto! (Spielbrett 4)

Name: _____

ein Eis	ein Hähnchen	ein Ei

Bonbons	Pommes Frites	ein Apfel

Lotto! (Spielbrett 1)

Name: _____

(etwas) Käse	Pommes Frites	ein Apfel
(etwas) Milch	(etwas) Schinken	ein Hähnchen

Lotto! (Spielbrett 2)

Name: _____

(etwas) Schinken	ein Kuchen	ein Ei
ein Hähnchen	eine Kartoffel	(etwas) Käse

Lotto! (Spielbrett 3)

Name: _____

Bonbons	ein Kuchen	(etwas) Brot
ein Eis	(etwas) Milch	ein Hähnchen

Lotto! (Spielbrett 4)

Name: _____

ein Eis	ein Hähnchen	ein Ei
Bonbons	Pommes Frites	ein Apfel

Im Klassenzimmer

Team 1 to win	Start on 2 or 7
Team 2 to win	Start on 1, 3, 4 or 12
Team 3 to win	Start on 3, 5, 7, 10 or 11
Team 4 to win	Start on 5, 7, 8 or 9
All teams to win	Start on 6

These numbers refer to the numbers on the left and right of the grid below.

Tick the white boxes in the grid as you call out the words.

					Winning team										
				2	1	2&3	2	3&4	All	1,3,4	4	4	3	3	2	
1	ein Buch	a book														1
2	ein Bleistift-spitzer	a pencil sharpener														2
3	ein Lineal	a ruler														3
4	eine Schultasche	a school bag														4
5	eine Schere	(some) scissors														5
6	ein Bleistift	a pencil														6
7	ein Radiergummi	a rubber														7
8	ein Heft	a workbook														8
9	ein Stift	a pen														9
10	ein Feder-mäppchen	a pencil case														10
11	ein Taschen-rechner	a calculator														11
12	ein Klebstoff	a glue stick														12
1	ein Buch	a book														1
2	ein Bleistift-spitzer	a pencil sharpener														2
3	ein Lineal	a ruler														3
4	eine Schultasche	a school bag														4
5	eine Schere	some scissors														5
6	ein Bleistift	a pencil														6
7	ein Radiergummi	a rubber														7
8	ein Heft	a workbook														8
9	ein Stift	a pen														9

Order of call

Lotto! (Spielbrett 1)　　　Name: _____

 Klebstoff |  |

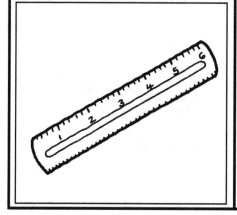 | Radier-gummi |

Deutsch-Lotto – Im Klassenzimmer

Lotto! (Spielbrett 2)　　　Name: _____

 |  |

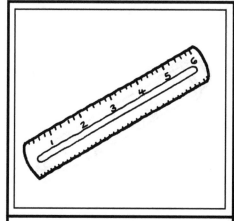 Klebstoff | 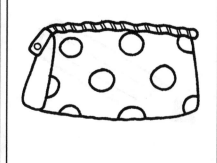 |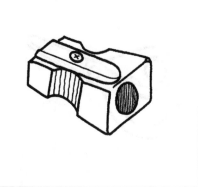

Deutsch-Lotto – Im Klassenzimmer

Lotto! (Spielbrett 3)   Name: _____

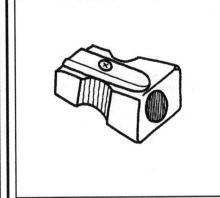

Deutsch-Lotto – Im Klassenzimmer

Lotto! (Spielbrett 4)   Name: _____

Deutsch-Lotto – Im Klassenzimmer

Lotto! (Spielbrett 1)   Name: _____

 ein Klebstoff	 ein Buch	 ein Taschen-rechner
 ein Lineal	 ein Radier-gummi	 eine Schere

Lotto! (Spielbrett 2)   Name: _____

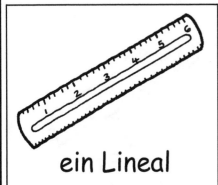 ein Lineal	 eine Schere	 ein Stift
 ein Klebstoff	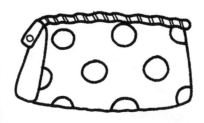 ein Feder-mäppchen	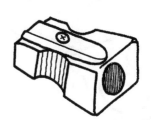 ein Bleistift-spitzer

Lotto! (Spielbrett 3)　Name: _____

 eine Schul-
tasche

 ein Feder-
mäppchen

 ein Bleistift-
spitzer

 ein Radiergummi

 ein Heft

 eine Schere

---

Lotto! (Spielbrett 4)　Name: _____

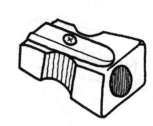

 ein Heft

 ein Buch

 ein Stift

 eine Schere

 ein Bleistift

 eine Schul-
tasche

Lotto! (Spielbrett 1) Name: _____

ein Klebstoff	ein Buch	ein Taschen-rechner
ein Lineal	ein Radier-gummi	eine Schere

Lotto! (Spielbrett 2) Name: _____

ein Lineal	eine Schere	ein Stift
ein Klebstoff	ein Feder-mäppchen	ein Bleistift-spitzer

Lotto! (Spielbrett 3)   Name: _____

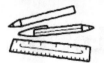

eine Schultasche	ein Feder-mäppchen	ein Bleistift-spitzer
ein Radier-gummi	ein Heft	eine Schere

Lotto! (Spielbrett 4)   Name: _____

ein Heft	ein Buch	ein Stift
eine Schere	ein Bleistift	eine Schul-tasche

Kleidung

Team 1 to win	Start on 2 or 7
Team 2 to win	Start on 1, 3, 4 or 12
Team 3 to win	Start on 3, 5, 7, 10 or 11
Team 4 to win	Start on 5, 7, 8 or 9
All teams to win	Start on 6

These numbers refer to the numbers on the left and right of the grid below.

Tick the white boxes in the grid as you call out the words.

Winning team

Order of call		German	English	2	1	2&3	2	3&4	All	1,3,4	4	4	3	3	2	
1		Schuhe	shoes													1
2		ein Pullover	a jumper													2
3		ein Kleid	a dress													3
4		eine Hose	(a pair of) trousers													4
5		eine Jeans	(a pair of) jeans													5
6		ein T-Shirt	a T-shirt													6
7		ein Hut	a hat													7
8		ein Rock	a skirt													8
9		ein Hemd	a shirt													9
10		eine Krawatte	a tie													10
11		Socken	socks													11
12		(ein Paar) Shorts	(a pair of) shorts													12
1		Schuhe	shoes													1
2		ein Pullover	a jumper													2
3		ein Kleid	a dress													3
4		eine Hose	(a pair of) trousers													4
5		eine Jeans	(a pair of) jeans													5
6		ein T-Shirt	a T-shirt													6
7		ein Hut	a hat													7
8		ein Rock	a skirt													8
9		ein Hemd	a shirt													9

Lotto! (Spielbrett 1)   Name: _____

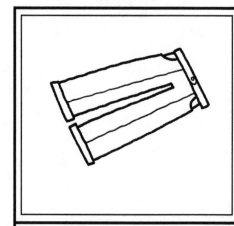  

 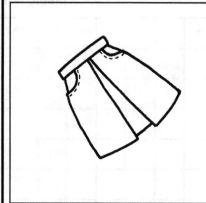 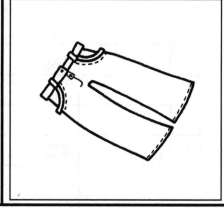

Lotto! (Spielbrett 2)   Name: _____

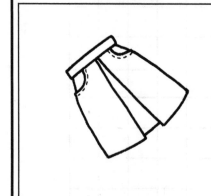  

  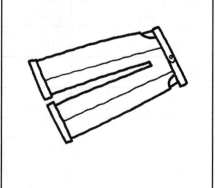

Lotto! (Spielbrett 3)

  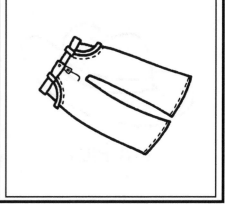

Deutsch-Lotto – Kleidung

Lotto! (Spielbrett 4)

Name: _____

Deutsch-Lotto – Kleidung

Lotto! (Spielbrett 1)

Name: _____

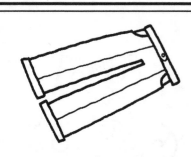

eine Hose

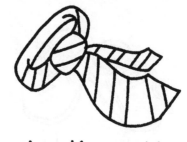

eine Krawatte

ein Pullover

ein Hut

ein Rock

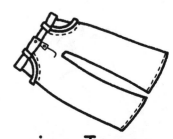

eine Jeans

Lotto! (Spielbrett 2)

Name: _____

ein Rock

Schuhe

ein Hemd

eine Jeans

ein T-Shirt

eine Hose

Lotto! (Spielbrett 3)   Name: _____

 **(ein Paar) Shorts**	 **Schuhe**	 **Socken**
 **ein Kleid**	 **ein Hut**	 **eine Jeans**

Lotto! (Spielbrett 4)   Name: _____

 **ein Kleid**	 **eine Jeans**	 **ein Hemd**
 **(ein Paar) Shorts**	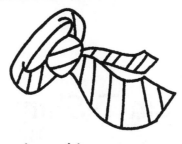 **eine Krawatte**	 **ein Pullover**

Lotto! (Spielbrett 1)

Name: _____

eine Hose	eine Krawatte	ein Pullover
ein Hut	ein Rock	eine Jeans

Lotto! (Spielbrett 2)

Name: _____

ein Rock	Schuhe	ein Hemd
eine Jeans	ein T-Shirt	eine Hose

Lotto! (Spielbrett 3)

Name: _____

(ein Paar) Shorts	Schuhe	Socken
ein Kleid	ein Hut	eine Jeans

Lotto! (Spielbrett 4)

Name: _____

ein Kleid	eine Jeans	ein Hemd
(ein Paar) Shorts	eine Krawatte	ein Pullover

Weihnachten

Team 1 to win	Start on 2 or 7
Team 2 to win	Start on 1, 3, 4 or 12
Team 3 to win	Start on 3, 5, 7, 10 or 11
Team 4 to win	Start on 5, 7, 8 or 9
All teams to win	Start on 6

These numbers refer to the numbers on the left and right of the grid below.

Tick the white boxes in the grid as you call out the words.

				Winning team												
				2	1	2&3	2	3&4	All	1,3,4	4	4	3	3	2	
Order of call	1	die Stechpalme	the holly													1
	2	der Truthahn	the turkey													2
	3	der Weihnachtsmann	Father Christmas													3
	4	der Schneemann	the snowman													4
	5	Fröhliche Weihnachten	Happy Christmas!													5
	6	der Weihnachts-baum	the Christmas tree													6
	7	25. Dezember	25th December													7
	8	der Stern	a star													8
	9	die Geschenke	presents													9
	10	die Krippe	the crib													10
	11	die Kerze	the candle													11
	12	das Rentier	the reindeer													12
	1	die Stechpalme	the holly													1
	2	der Truthahn	the turkey													2
	3	der Wiehnachtsmann	Father Christmas													3
	4	der Schneemann	the snowman													4
	5	Fröhliche Weihnachten	Happy Christmas													5
	6	der Weihnachts-baum	the Christmas tree													6
	7	25. Dezember	25th December													7
	8	der Stern	the star													8
	9	die Geschenke	presents													9

We have used the definite article (der, die, das) for the Christmas words (instead of the indefinite article as used for other topics) as it seemed more appropriate. This could provide the stimulus for getting children to practise both forms.

Lotto! (Spielbrett 1)   Name: _____

Lotto! (Spielbrett 2)   Name: _____

Lotto! (Spielbrett 3)   Name: _____

Lotto! (Spielbrett 4)   Name: _____

der Schneemann

die Krippe

der Truthahn

25. Dezember

der Stern

Lotto! (Spielbrett 2)

Name: _____

der Stern

die Stechpalme

die Geschenke

der Weihnachtsbaum

der Schneemann

Lotto! (Spielbrett 3)

Name: _____

das Rentier

die Stechpalme

die Kerze

der Weihnachtsmann

25. Dezember

Lotto! (Spielbrett 4)

Name: _____

der Weihnachtsmann

die Geschenke

das Rentier

die Krippe

der Truthahn

Lotto! (Spielbrett 1)

Name: _____

der Schneemann	die Krippe	der Truthahn
25. Dezember	der Stern	Fröhliche Weihnachten

Lotto! (Spielbrett 2)

Name: _____

der Stern	die Stechpalme	die Geschenke
Fröhliche Weihnachten	der Weihnachtsbaum	der Schneemann

Lotto! (Spielbrett 3)

Name: _____

das Rentier	die Stechpalme	die Kerze
der Weih-nachtsmann	25. Dezember	Fröhliche Weihnachten

Lotto! (Spielbrett 4)

Name: _____

der Weih-nachtsmann	Fröhliche Weihnachten	die Geschenke
das Rentier	die Krippe	der Truthahn

Lotto! (Spielbrett   )   Name: _____

Lotto! (Spielbrett   )   Name: _____

List of vocabulary used in the games

Die Zahlen 1–12

eins	1
zwei	2
drei	3
vier	4
fünf	5
sechs	6
sieben	7
acht	8
neun	9
zehn	10
elf	11
zwölf	12

Die Zahlen 1–60

sieben	7
zwölf	12
fünfzehn	15
neunzehn	19
sechsundzwanzig	26
vierunddreißig	34
fünfunddreißig	35
einundvierzig	41
zweiundvierzig	42
fünfzig	50
achtundfünfzig	58
sechzig	60

Tiere

eine Ente	a duck
eine Katze	a cat
ein Pferd	a horse
ein Hund	a dog
ein Schwein	a pig
ein Meerschweinchen	a Guinea pig
ein Hamster	a hamster
ein Kaninchen	a rabbit
ein Goldfisch	a goldfish
eine Henne	a hen
eine Maus	a mouse
eine Kuh	a cow

Essen

Bonbons	sweets
Pomme Frites	chips
(etwas) Käse	(some) cheese
ein Kuchen	a cake
ein Eis	an ice-cream
ein Ei	an egg
(etwas) Brot	(some) bread
ein Hähnchen	a chicken
ein Apfel	an apple
(etwas) Schinken	(some) ham
eine Kartoffel	a potato
(etwas) Milch	(some) milk

Im Klassenzimmer

ein Klebstoff	a glue stick
ein Heft	a workbook
ein Taschenrechner	a calculator
eine Schultasche	a school bag
eine Schere	(some) scissors
ein Bleistift	a pencil
ein Radiergummi	a rubber
ein Buch	a book
ein Lineal	a ruler
ein Stift	a pen
ein Bleistiftspitzer	a pencil sharpener
ein Federmäppchen	a pencil case

Kleidung

ein Hut	a hat
Socken	socks
Schuhe	shoes
ein Hemd	a shirt
eine Krawatte	a tie
eine Jeans	(a pair of) jeans
ein Kleid	a dress
eine Hose	(a pair of) trousers
ein Pullover	a jumper
ein Rock	a skirt
(ein Paar) Shorts	(a pair of) shorts
ein T-Shirt	a T-shirt

Weihnachten

die Stechpalme	the holly
der Truthahn	the turkey
der Weihnachtsmann	Father Christmas
Fröhliche Weihnachten	Happy Christmas
der Weihnachtsbaum	the Christmas tree
25. Dezember	25th December
der Stern	the star
die Geschenke	presents
die Krippe	the crib
die Kerze	the candle
das Rentier	the reindeer
der Schneemann	the snowman

Printed in the USA
CPSIA information can be obtained
at www.ICGtesting.com
LVHW071648161223
766679LV00018B/1247